Christian Crafts Paper Bag Puppets

by Susan J. Stegenga

illustrated by Vanessa Filkins

Cover by Vanessa Filkins

Shining Star Publications, Copyright © 1990

A Division of Good Apple, Inc.

ISBN No. 0-86653-552-7

Standard Subject Code TA ac

Printing No. 98

Shining Star Publications
A Division of Good Apple, Inc.
1204 Buchanan St., Box 299
Carthage, IL 62321-0299

Unless otherwise indicated, the King James Version of the Bible was used in preparing the activities in this book.

TABLE OF CONTENTS

DEDICATION

This book is lovingly dedicated to my entire family and to the many children who have been my "teachers."

This book is especially written in memory of my dear uncle, Edwin M. Luidens, who went home to be with the Lord, on May 12, 1989. I hope that his grandchildren will enjoy learning more about our Lord through this book.

We miss you, Uncle Ed!

TEACHING TIPS

TO THE TEACHER OR PARENT:

This book has been created to educate as well as entertain young children. The basic focus is for younger children, but older youngsters will also enjoy making and using these puppets.

Use these puppets as visual aids while you tell favorite Bible stories to children. Or, you can help children decorate these puppets so they act out and review Bible stories.

General ideas for making and using the puppets are suggested on these introductory pages. Other more specific ideas are suggested throughout the book.

OVERALL BASIC MATERIALS NEEDED:

A Bible or children's Bible story/picture book

Copies of puppet heads, mouths, props, and accessories

Crayons or felt-tip marking pens

Scissors (blunt-edged type if young children will cut out the pieces themselves)

Glue, gluestick, or paste

Lunch-size paper bags (exception: large grocery bag needed for Goliath, the Giant)

GENERAL OPTIONAL MATERIALS:

Yarn, cotton, or fake fur to make hair, beards, and animal fur on puppets

Fabric scraps to make clothing, head coverings, blankets, and tents for puppets

A box or table turned on its side as a stage (A stage is not necessary but should be kept simple if used.)

PLANNING/MAKING THE PUPPETS

1. Choose the characters, accessories, props, and other materials you will need to tell a particular Bible story. Refer to the charts (beginning on page 57) of possible stories and suggestions to give you ideas for planning. The people puppets represent various age groups from babies to elderly folks. Thus, these puppets are designed to be used as the characters in many different stories. If several characters of the same age and gender are to be used in one specific story, the puppets can be decorated so each one looks unique. For example, two boy puppets can have different colored clothing and hair so they both look different. There is also a large puppet head provided to make Goliath, the Giant. In addition, there are many different animal patterns in the book. At the end of the book are several pages providing props and various costume accessories.

2. Make copies of the puppets' heads, mouths, accessories, and props. Do so by using a copy machine or by tracing the images onto white paper. (If you don't cut apart the actual pages of this book, you can use the original pages again to make as many copies as you need.)

3. Color the puppet heads, mouths, accessories, and props.

4. Cut out the pieces to make the puppets.

5. Glue or paste the parts of the puppets on the paper bags as shown on the illustrations in the book.

6. Decorate the puppets by gluing or pasting on any optional materials.

USING THE PUPPETS:

1. Read the story from the Bible or a Bible storybook to become familiar with the important facts. Manipulate the puppets to retell the story while the children listen and watch. Or, whenever possible, encourage the children to move the puppets and improvise conversations themselves to tell the story. Help the youngsters think about the basic emotions causing the characters to act as they do. Discuss feelings such as happiness, sadness, trust, fear, and anger as these emotions relate to the story. Encourage spontaneous creative dramatics based upon the Bible facts.

2. Slip one puppet over each hand. One person can operate two puppets at the same time to simulate a two-way conversation. Very young children will find it easier to operate only one puppet at a time.

3. The person manipulating the puppet should speak clearly while moving his or her hand to open the puppet's mouth. A puppeteer does not need to try to be a ventriloquist. Young children usually don't even notice that a real person is actually speaking for the puppet, even when the person is in full view.

4. You may wish to decorate a complete basic set of puppets to have readily available to tell a variety of Bible stories. (You can store puppets in a flat box when not in use. Thus, storage of these puppets requires very little space.)

Have fun with your "puppet parade!"

SS1881

BABY

SS1881

BABY PUPPET

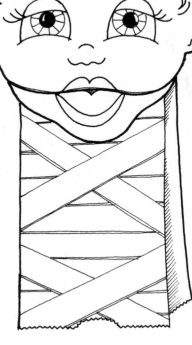

BIBLE STORIES:

Baby Moses in the Basket . . . Exodus 2:1-10

Christmas (Baby Jesus) . . . Matthew 1-2; Luke 2:1-20

Jesus Loves the Children . . . Matthew 18:1-5; 19:13-15;
Mark 9:33-37

MATERIALS:

A Bible or children's Bible story/picture book

Copy of puppet head and mouth

Crayons or felt-tip marking pens

Scissors

Glue, gluestick, or paste

Lunch-size paper bag

Glue top of head here.

Baby Jesus' "swaddling clothes" (white tape or strips of white fabric)

OPTIONAL MATERIALS:

For Baby Jesus: white medical tape or strips of white fabric (such as from an old cotton sheet)

HOW TO MAKE PUPPET:

1. Color the puppet's head and mouth.

2. Cut out the pieces.

3. Glue or paste the parts on the paper bag as shown in the picture.

OPTIONAL/SPECIAL INSTRUCTIONS:

Make "swaddling clothes" for Baby Jesus by applying white tape or gluing on strips of white fabric.

  SS1881

GIRL

SS1881

GIRL PUPPET

BIBLE STORIES:

Baby Moses in the Basket (Sister Miriam) . . . Exodus 2:1-10

Jesus Loves the Children . . . Matthew 18:1-5; 19:13-15; Mark 9:33-37

Jesus Feeds the Multitude . . . John 6:1-14

Palm Sunday . . . Matthew 21:1-11; Mark 11:1-10; Luke 19:28-38;
John 12:12-15

MATERIALS:

A Bible or children's Bible story/picture book

Copy of puppet head and mouth

Crayons or felt-tip marking pens

Scissors

Glue, gluestick, or paste

Lunch-size paper bag

Glue top of head here.

OPTIONAL MATERIALS:

Yarn
Fabric scraps

HOW TO MAKE PUPPET:

1. Color the puppet's head and mouth.

2. Cut out the pieces.

3. Glue or paste the parts on the paper bag as shown in the picture.

OPTIONAL/SPECIAL INSTRUCTIONS:

Glue yarn onto the girl's hair.

Glue scraps of fabric onto the girl's headband and onto the bag as clothing.

Shining Star Publications, Copyright © 1990, A division of Good Apple, Inc.

SS1881

BOY

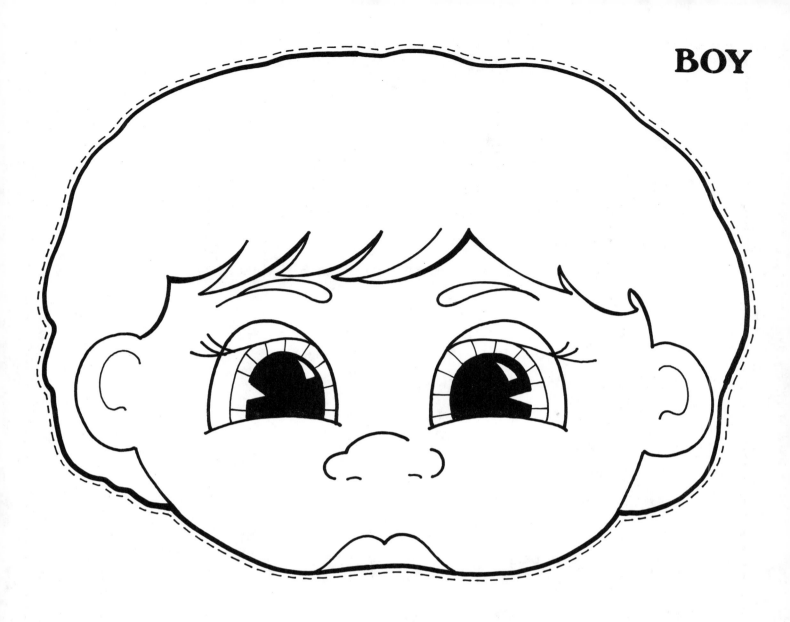

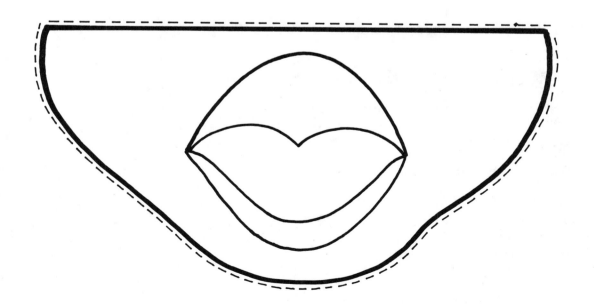

SS1881

BOY PUPPET

BIBLE STORIES:

The Garden of Eden (Cain and Abel) . . . Genesis 1:24-31; 2:18-23; 4:2-3

David and Goliath . . . I Samuel 17

Jesus Loves the Children . . . Matthew 18:1-5; 19:13-15; Mark 9:33-37

Jesus Feeds the Multitude . . . John 6:1-14

Palm Sunday . . . Matthew 21:1-11; Mark 11:1-10; Luke 19:28-38;
John 12:12-15

MATERIALS:

A Bible or children's Bible story/picture book

Copy of puppet head and mouth

Crayons or felt-tip marking pens

Scissors

Glue, gluestick, or paste

Lunch-size paper bag

Glue top of head here.

OPTIONAL MATERIALS:

Yarn
Fabric scraps

HOW TO MAKE PUPPET:

1. Color the puppet's head and mouth.

2. Cut out the pieces.

3. Glue or paste the parts on the paper bag as shown in the picture.

OPTIONAL/SPECIAL INSTRUCTIONS:

Glue yarn onto the boy's hair.

Glue scraps of fabric onto the boy's headband and onto the bag as clothing.

Shining Star Publications, Copyright © 1990, A division of Good Apple, Inc.   SS1881

TEENAGE
GIRL OR
YOUNG WOMAN

TEENAGE GIRL OR YOUNG WOMAN PUPPET

BIBLE STORIES:

The Garden of Eden (Eve) . . . Genesis 1:24-31; 2:18-23; 4:2-3

Noah's Ark . . . Genesis 6-9:1-19

Baby Moses in the Basket . . . Exodus 2:1-10

Christmas (Mother Mary) . . . Matthew 1-2; Luke 2:1-20

Jesus Feeds the Multitude . . . John 6:1-14

Palm Sunday . . . Matthew 21:1-11; Mark 11:1-10; Luke 19:28-38;
        John 12:12-15

Easter . . . Matthew 28:1-10; Mark 16; Luke 24:1-12; John 20:1-18

See index chart and the Bible for other stories

MATERIALS:

A Bible or children's Bible story/picture book

Copy of puppet head and mouth

Crayons or felt-tip marking pens

Scissors

Glue, gluestick, or paste

Lunch-size paper bag

Glue top of head here.

OPTIONAL MATERIALS:

Yarn
Fabric scraps

HOW TO MAKE PUPPET:

1. Color the puppet's head and mouth.

2. Cut out the pieces.

3. Glue or paste the parts on the paper bag as shown in the picture.

4. Glue yarn onto the woman's hair.

5. Glue scraps of fabric onto the bag as clothing.

SS1881

TEENAGE BOY OR YOUNG MAN

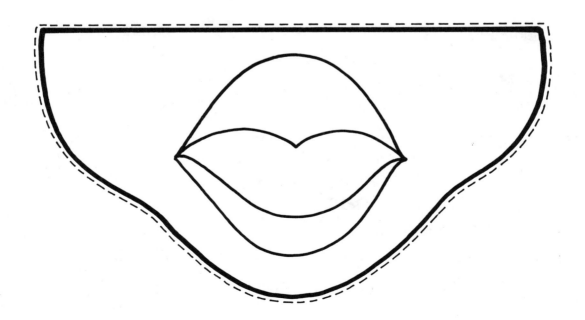

13

SS1881

TEENAGE BOY OR YOUNG MAN PUPPET

BIBLE STORIES:

The Garden of Eden (Adam) . . . Genesis 1:24-31; 2:18-23; 4:2-3

Noah's Ark . . . Genesis 6-9:1-19

Daniel in the Lion's Den . . . Daniel 6

Christmas . . . Matthew 1-2; Luke 2:1-20

The Prodigal Son . . . Luke 15:11-32

Palm Sunday . . . Matthew 21:1-11; Mark 11:1-10; Luke 19:28-38;
John 12:12-15

See index chart and the Bible for other stories

MATERIALS:

A Bible or children's Bible story/picture book

Copy of puppet head and mouth

Crayons or felt-tip marking pens

Scissors

Glue, gluestick, or paste

Lunch-size paper bag

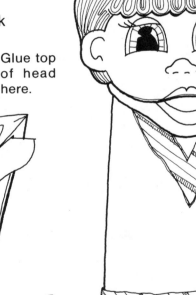

Glue top of head here.

OPTIONAL MATERIALS:

Yarn
Fabric scraps

HOW TO MAKE PUPPET:

1. Color the puppet's head and mouth.
2. Cut out the pieces.
3. Glue or paste the parts on the paper bag as shown in the picture.

OPTIONAL/SPECIAL INSTRUCTIONS:

Glue yarn onto the man's hair.

Glue scraps of fabric onto the bag as clothing.

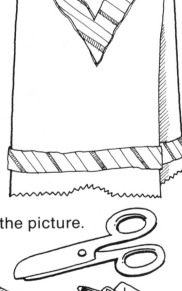

 SS1881

MIDDLE-AGED OR OLDER WOMAN

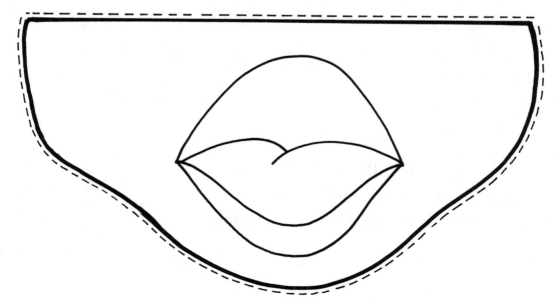

15

SS1881

MIDDLE-AGED OR OLDER WOMAN PUPPET

BIBLE STORIES:

Noah's Ark . . . Genesis 6-9:1-19

Palm Sunday . . . Matthew 21:1-11; Mark 11:1-10; Luke 19:28-38;
John 12:12-15

Easter . . . Matthew 28:1-10; Mark 16; Luke 24:1-12; John 20:1-18

See index chart and the Bible for other stories

MATERIALS:

A Bible or children's Bible story/picture book

Copy of puppet head and mouth

Crayons or felt-tip marking pens

Scissors

Glue, gluestick, or paste

Lunch-size paper bag

Glue top of head here.

OPTIONAL MATERIALS:

Yarn or cotton balls
Fabric scraps

HOW TO MAKE PUPPET:

1. Color the puppet's head and mouth.

2. Cut out the pieces.

3. Glue or paste the parts on the paper bag as shown in the picture.

OPTIONAL/SPECIAL INSTRUCTIONS:

Glue yarn or cotton onto the woman's hair.

Glue scraps of fabric onto the bag as clothing.

SS1881

MIDDLE-AGED
OR OLDER
MAN OR
JESUS

17

SS1881

MIDDLE-AGED OR OLDER MAN OR JESUS PUPPET

BIBLE STORIES:

Noah's Ark . . . Genesis 6-9:1-19

David and Goliath . . . I Samuel 17

The Lord Is My Shepherd . . . Psalm 23

Jesus Feeds the Multitude . . . John 6:1-14

Palm Sunday . . . Matthew 21:1-11; Mark 11:1-10;
Luke 19:28-38; John 12:12-15

Easter . . . Matthew 28:1-10; Mark 16; Luke 24:1-12;
John 20:1-18

See index chart and the Bible for other stories

MATERIALS:

A Bible or children's Bible story/picture book

Copy of puppet head and mouth

Crayons or felt-tip marking pens

Scissors

Glue, gluestick, or paste

Lunch-size paper bag

Glue top of head here.

OPTIONAL MATERIALS:

Yarn or cotton balls

Fabric scraps

HOW TO MAKE PUPPET:

1. Color the puppet's head and mouth.
2. Cut out the pieces.
3. Glue or paste the parts on the paper bag as shown in the picture.

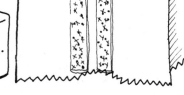

OPTIONAL/SPECIAL INSTRUCTIONS:

Glue yarn or cotton onto the man's hair, eyebrows, beard, and mustache. (Jesus should have hair that is a younger looking hair color such as brown, but an older man can have white hair made from cotton.)

Glue scraps of fabric onto the bag as clothing.

SS1881

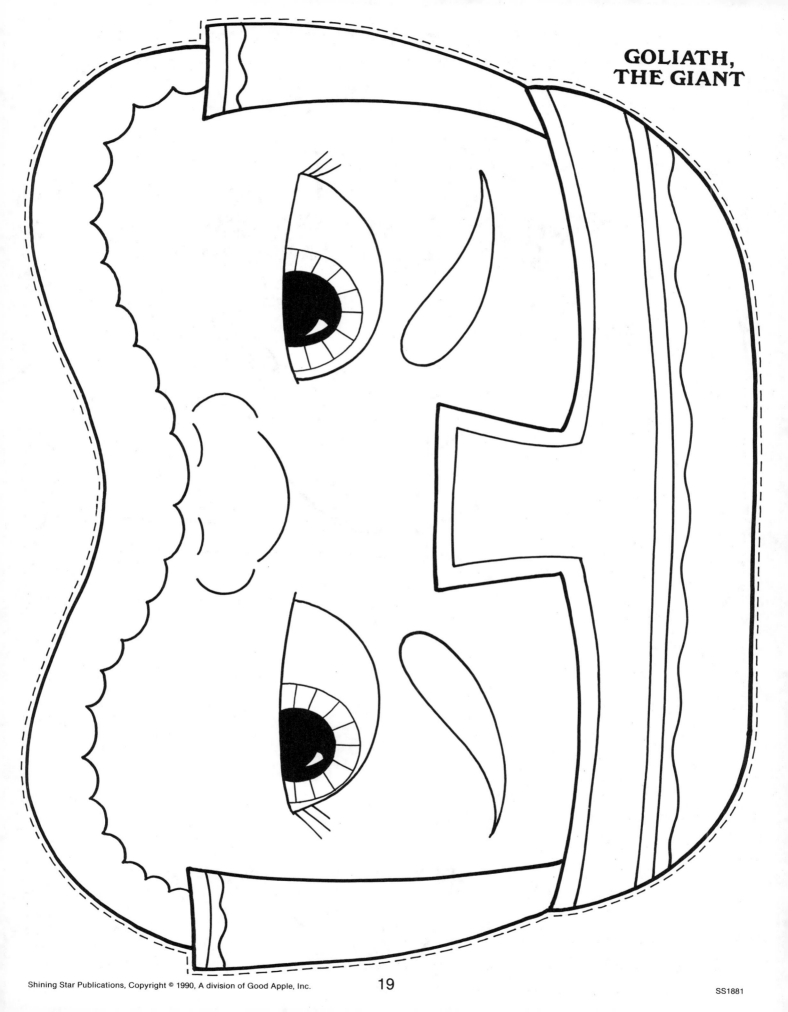

GOLIATH,
THE GIANT

SS1881

GOLIATH'S MOUTH AND BEARD

SS1881

GOLIATH, THE GIANT PUPPET

BIBLE STORIES:

David and Goliath . . . I Samuel 17

MATERIALS:

A Bible or children's Bible story/picture book

Copy of puppet head and mouth

Crayons or felt-tip marking pens

Scissors

Glue, gluestick, or paste

Large-size grocery bag

OPTIONAL MATERIALS:

Yarn

Glitter, sequins, foil scraps, or metallic-colored crayons or ink pens

HOW TO MAKE PUPPET:

1. Color the puppet's head and mouth.

2. Cut out the pieces.

3. Glue or paste the parts on the paper bag as shown in the picture.

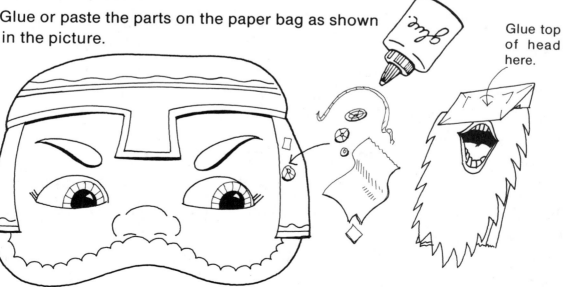

Glue top of head here.

Shining Star Publications, Copyright © 1990, A division of Good Apple, Inc. SS1881

DAVID AND GOLIATH PUPPETS

Goliath, the Giant

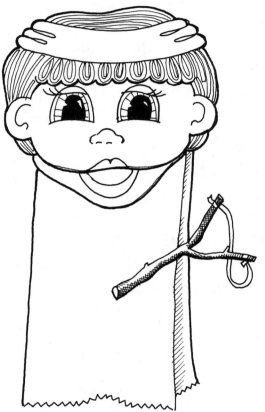

David made from
a "boy" puppet

Slingshot made from
forked twig and large
rubber band or elastic

OPTIONAL/SPECIAL INSTRUCTIONS:

Glue scraps of yarn onto Goliath's hair, eyebrows, mustache, and beard.

Glue glitter, sequins, or scraps of foil onto Goliath's helmet. Or, color it with metallic crayons or ink-pens.

Act out the story by using the Goliath puppet with a boy puppet decorated to be David and his slingshot.

SS1881

LAMB

23

SS1881

LAMB PUPPET

BIBLE STORIES:

The Garden of Eden (God Created Animals; The Animals Are Named) . . . Genesis 1:24-28; 2:19-20

Noah's Ark . . . Genesis 6-9:1-19

David and Goliath (David, the Shepherd Boy) . . . I Samuel 17

The Lord Is My Shepherd . . . Psalm 23

Christmas . . . Matthew 1-2; Luke 2:1-20

The Lost Sheep . . . Matthew 18:12-14; Luke 15:3-7

MATERIALS:

A Bible or children's Bible story/picture book

Copy of puppet head and mouth

Crayons or felt-tip marking pens

Scissors

Glue, gluestick, or paste

Lunch-size paper bag

Glue top of head here.

OPTIONAL MATERIALS:

Cotton balls

HOW TO MAKE PUPPET:

1. Color the puppet's head and mouth.

2. Cut out the pieces.

3. Glue or paste the parts on the paper bag as shown in the picture.

OPTIONAL/SPECIAL INSTRUCTIONS:

Glue bits of cotton onto the lamb's head and the paper bag as fur and a tail.

Make two sheep for Noah's Ark story.

SS1881

DONKEY

SS1881

DONKEY PUPPET

BIBLE STORIES:

The Garden of Eden (God Created Animals; The Animals Are Named) . . .
   Genesis 1:24-28; 2:19-20

Noah's Ark . . . Genesis 6-9:1-19

Christmas . . . Matthew 1-2; Luke 2:1-20

Palm Sunday . . . Matthew 21:1-11; Mark 11:1-10;
   Luke 19:28-38; John 12:12-15

MATERIALS:

A Bible or children's Bible story/picture book

Copy of puppet head and mouth

Crayons or felt-tip marking pens

Scissors

Glue, gluestick, or paste

Lunch-size paper bag

OPTIONAL MATERIALS:

Yarn or fake fur

Clear (Scotch) tape

Glue top of head here.

HOW TO MAKE PUPPET:

1. Color the puppet's head and mouth.
2. Cut out the pieces.
3. Glue or paste the parts on the paper bag as shown in the picture.

OPTIONAL/SPECIAL INSTRUCTIONS:

Glue or tape bits of yarn or fake fur onto the mane and on the back as a tail.

Tape a piece of yarn approximately 14 inches long around the donkey's head to be its reins.

Make two donkeys for the Noah's Ark story.

 SS1881

CAMEL

27

SS1881

CAMEL PUPPET

BIBLE STORIES:

The Garden of Eden (God Created Animals; The Animals Are Named) . . .
Genesis 1:24-28; 2:19-20

Noah's Ark . . . Genesis 6-9:1-19

Christmas . . . Matthew 1-2; Luke 2:1-20

MATERIALS:

A Bible or children's Bible story/picture book

Copy of puppet head and mouth

Crayons or felt-tip marking pens

Scissors

Glue, gluestick, or paste

Lunch-size paper bag

OPTIONAL MATERIALS:

Yarn

Glue top of head here.

HOW TO MAKE PUPPET:

1. Color the puppet's head and mouth.

2. Cut out the pieces.

3. Glue or paste the parts on the paper bag as shown in the picture.

OPTIONAL/SPECIAL INSTRUCTIONS:

Glue bits of yarn onto the tassels on the camel's harness.
Make two camels for the Noah's Ark story.

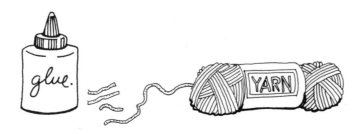

SS1881

COW

SS1881

COW PUPPET

BIBLE STORIES:

The Garden of Eden (God Created Animals; The Animals Are Named) . . .
   Genesis 1:24-28; 2:19-20

Noah's Ark . . . Genesis 6-9:1-19

Christmas . . . Matthew 1-2; Luke 2:1-20

MATERIALS:

A Bible or children's Bible story/picture book

Copy of puppet head and mouth

Crayons or felt-tip marking pens

Scissors

Glue, gluestick, or paste

Lunch-size paper bag

OPTIONAL MATERIALS:

Yarn or fake fur

HOW TO MAKE PUPPET:

1. Color the puppet's head and mouth.

2. Cut out the pieces.

3. Glue or paste the parts on the paper bag as shown in the picture.

OPTIONAL/SPECIAL INSTRUCTIONS:

Glue bits of yarn or fake fur onto the cow's head.

Make two cows for the Noah's Ark story.

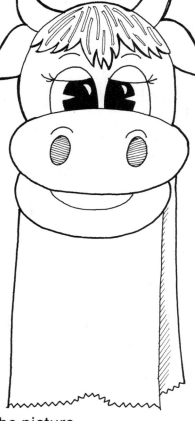

Glue top of head here.

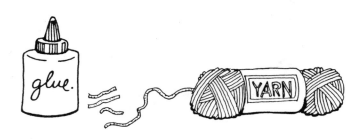

Shining Star Publications, Copyright © 1990, A division of Good Apple, Inc.   SS1881

GOAT

SS1881

GOAT PUPPET

BIBLE STORIES:

The Garden of Eden (God Created Animals; The Animals Are Named) . . .
   Genesis 1:24-28; 2:19-20

Noah's Ark . . . Genesis 6-9:1-19

Christmas . . . Matthew 1-2; Luke 2:1-20

MATERIALS:

A Bible or children's Bible story/picture book

Copy of puppet head and mouth

Crayons or felt-tip marking pens

Scissors

Glue, gluestick, or paste

Lunch-size paper bag

OPTIONAL MATERIALS:

Yarn or fake fur

Glue top of head here.

HOW TO MAKE PUPPET:

1. Color the puppet's head and mouth.
2. Cut out the pieces.
3. Glue or paste the parts on the paper bag as shown in the picture.

OPTIONAL/SPECIAL INSTRUCTIONS:

Glue bits of yarn or fake fur onto the goat's ears and beard.

Make two goats for the Noah's Ark story.

SS1881

PIG

SS1881

PIG PUPPET

BIBLE STORIES:

The Garden of Eden (God Created Animals; The Animals Are Named) . . .
  Genesis 1:24-28; 2:19-20

Noah's Ark . . . Genesis 6-9:1-19

The Prodigal Son . . . Luke 15:11-32

MATERIALS:

A Bible or children's Bible story/picture book

Copy of puppet head and mouth

Crayons or felt-tip marking pens

Scissors

Glue, gluestick, or paste

Lunch-size paper bag

OPTIONAL MATERIALS:

Scrap of pink or tan paper or a
  chenille wire (pipe cleaner)

Clear (Scotch) tape

Glue top
of head
here.

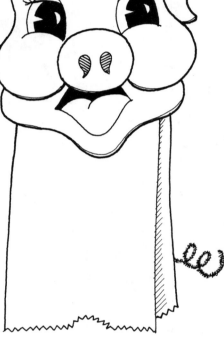

HOW TO MAKE PUPPET:

1. Color the puppet's head and mouth.

2. Cut out the pieces.

3. Glue or paste the parts on the paper bag as shown in the picture.

OPTIONAL/SPECIAL INSTRUCTIONS:

Twist a chenille wire into a coiled shape or cut a piece of pink paper to be the pig's curled tail.

Tape the tail to the back of the pig.

Make two pigs for the Noah's Ark story.

SS1881

CAT

SS1881

CAT PUPPET

BIBLE STORIES:

The Garden of Eden (God Created Animals; The Animals Are Named) . . .
Genesis 1:24-28; 2:19-20

Noah's Ark . . . Genesis 6-9:1-19

MATERIALS:

A Bible or children's Bible story/picture book

Copy of puppet head and mouth

Crayons or felt-tip marking pens

Scissors

Glue, gluestick, or paste

Lunch-size paper bag

OPTIONAL MATERIALS:

Yarn
Scrap of paper
Clear (Scotch) tape

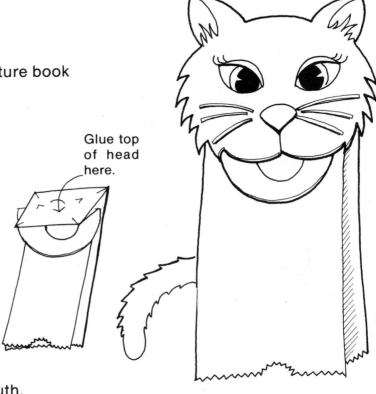

Glue top of head here.

HOW TO MAKE PUPPET:

1. Color the puppet's head and mouth.

2. Cut out the pieces.

3. Glue or paste the parts on the paper bag as shown in the picture.

OPTIONAL/SPECIAL INSTRUCTIONS:

Glue bits of yarn onto the cat's whiskers.

Cut out a paper tail and tape it to the back of the cat.

Make two cats for the Noah's Ark story.

SS1881

DOG

                    SS1881

DOG PUPPET

BIBLE STORIES:

The Garden of Eden (God Created Animals; The Animals Are Named) . . .
   Genesis 1:24-28; 2:19-20

Noah's Ark . . . Genesis 6-9:1-19

MATERIALS:

A Bible or children's Bible story/picture book

Copy of puppet head and mouth

Crayons or felt-tip marking pens

Scissors

Glue, gluestick, or paste

Lunch-size paper bag

OPTIONAL MATERIALS:

Fake fur

Scrap of paper

Clear (Scotch) tape

Glue top of head here.

HOW TO MAKE PUPPET:

1. Color the puppet's head and mouth.

2. Cut out the pieces.

3. Glue or paste the parts on the paper bag as shown in the picture.

OPTIONAL/SPECIAL INSTRUCTIONS:

Glue bits of fake fur onto the dog's ears.

Cut out a paper tail and tape it to the back of the dog.

Make two dogs for the Noah's Ark story.

glue.

SS1881

DUCK

SS1881

DUCK PUPPET

BIBLE STORIES:

The Garden of Eden (God Created Animals; The Animals Are Named) . . .
   Genesis 1:24-28; 2:19-20

Noah's Ark . . . Genesis 6-9:1-19

MATERIALS:

A Bible or children's Bible story/picture book

Copy of puppet head and mouth

Crayons or felt-tip marking pens

Scissors

Glue, gluestick, or paste

Lunch-size paper bag

Glue top
of head
here.

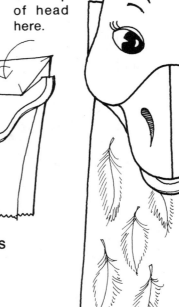

OPTIONAL MATERIALS:

Yellow or natural-colored (brown, tan, etc.) feathers

Clear (Scotch) tape

HOW TO MAKE PUPPET:

1. Color the puppet's head and mouth.

2. Cut out the pieces.

3. Glue or paste the parts on the paper bag as shown in the picture.

OPTIONAL/SPECIAL INSTRUCTIONS:

Glue or tape feathers to the front and back of the paper bag.

Make two ducks for the Noah's Ark story.

SS1881

BEAR

BEAR PUPPET

BIBLE STORIES:

The Garden of Eden (God Created Animals; The Animals Are Named) . . .
   Genesis 1:24-28; 2:19-20

Noah's Ark . . . Genesis 6-9:1-19

MATERIALS:

A Bible or children's Bible story/picture book

Copy of puppet head and mouth

Crayons or felt-tip marking pens

Scissors

Glue, gluestick, or paste

Lunch-size paper bag

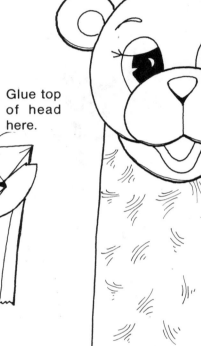

Glue top
of head
here.

OPTIONAL MATERIALS:

Fake fur

HOW TO MAKE PUPPET:

1. Color the puppet's head and mouth.

2. Cut out the pieces.

3. Glue or paste the parts on the paper bag as shown in the picture.

OPTIONAL/SPECIAL INSTRUCTIONS:

Glue bits of fake fur to the front and back of the paper bag.

Make two bears for the Noah's Ark story.

SS1881

MONKEY

SS1881

MONKEY PUPPET

BIBLE STORIES:

The Garden of Eden (God Created Animals; The Animals Are Named) . . . Genesis 1:24-28; 2:19-20

Noah's Ark . . . Genesis 6-9:1-19

MATERIALS:

A Bible or children's Bible story/picture book

Copy of puppet head and mouth

Crayons or felt-tip marking pens

Scissors

Glue, gluestick, or paste

Lunch-size paper bag

OPTIONAL MATERIALS:

Fake fur

Scrap of paper

Clear (Scotch) tape

Glue top of head here.

HOW TO MAKE PUPPET:

1. Color the puppet's head and mouth.
2. Cut out the pieces.
3. Glue or paste the parts on the paper bag as shown in the picture.

OPTIONAL/SPECIAL INSTRUCTIONS:

Glue bits of fake fur around the monkey's face.

Cut out a long, curled tail from paper and tape it to the back of the monkey.

Make two monkeys for the Noah's Ark story.

SS1881

TIGER

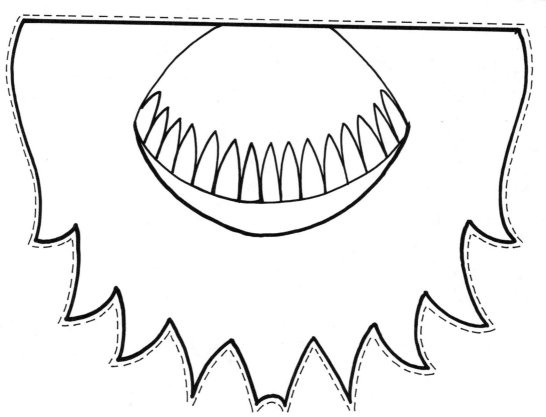

SS1881

TIGER PUPPET

BIBLE STORIES:

The Garden of Eden (God Created Animals; The Animals Are Named) . . .
Genesis 1:24-28; 2:19-20

Noah's Ark . . . Genesis 6-9:1-19

MATERIALS:

A Bible or children's Bible story/picture book

Copy of puppet head and mouth

Crayons or felt-tip marking pens

Scissors

Glue, gluestick, or paste

Lunch-size paper bag

Glue top of head here.

OPTIONAL MATERIALS:

Scrap of paper

Clear (Scotch) tape

HOW TO MAKE PUPPET:

1. Color the puppet's head and mouth.

2. Cut out the pieces.

3. Glue or paste the parts on the paper bag as shown in the picture.

OPTIONAL/SPECIAL INSTRUCTIONS:

Cut out a paper tail and draw black stripes on it. Tape the tail to the back of the tiger.

Make two tigers for the Noah's Ark story.

Shining Star Publications, Copyright © 1990, A division of Good Apple, Inc.   SS1881

LION

47

SS1881

LION PUPPET

BIBLE STORIES:

The Garden of Eden (God Created Animals; The Animals Are Named) . . .
Genesis 1:24-28; 2:19-20

Noah's Ark . . . Genesis 6-9:1-19

Daniel in the Lion's Den . . . Daniel 6

MATERIALS:

A Bible or children's Bible story/picture book

Copy of puppet head and mouth

Crayons or felt-tip marking pens

Scissors

Glue, gluestick, or paste

Lunch-size paper bag

OPTIONAL MATERIALS:

Scrap of paper

Clear (Scotch) tape

Yarn or fake fur

Glue top of head here.

HOW TO MAKE PUPPET:

1. Color the puppet's head and mouth.

2. Cut out the pieces.

3. Glue or paste the parts on the paper bag as shown in the picture.

OPTIONAL/SPECIAL INSTRUCTIONS:

Cut out a paper tail and tape it to the back of the lion.

Cut the end of the paper tail to look fringed or glue on bits of yarn or fake fur.

Glue bits of yarn or fake fur to the lion's mane.

Make two lions for the Noah's Ark story.

glue

YARN

Shining Star Publications, Copyright © 1990, A division of Good Apple, Inc.   SS1881

ELEPHANT

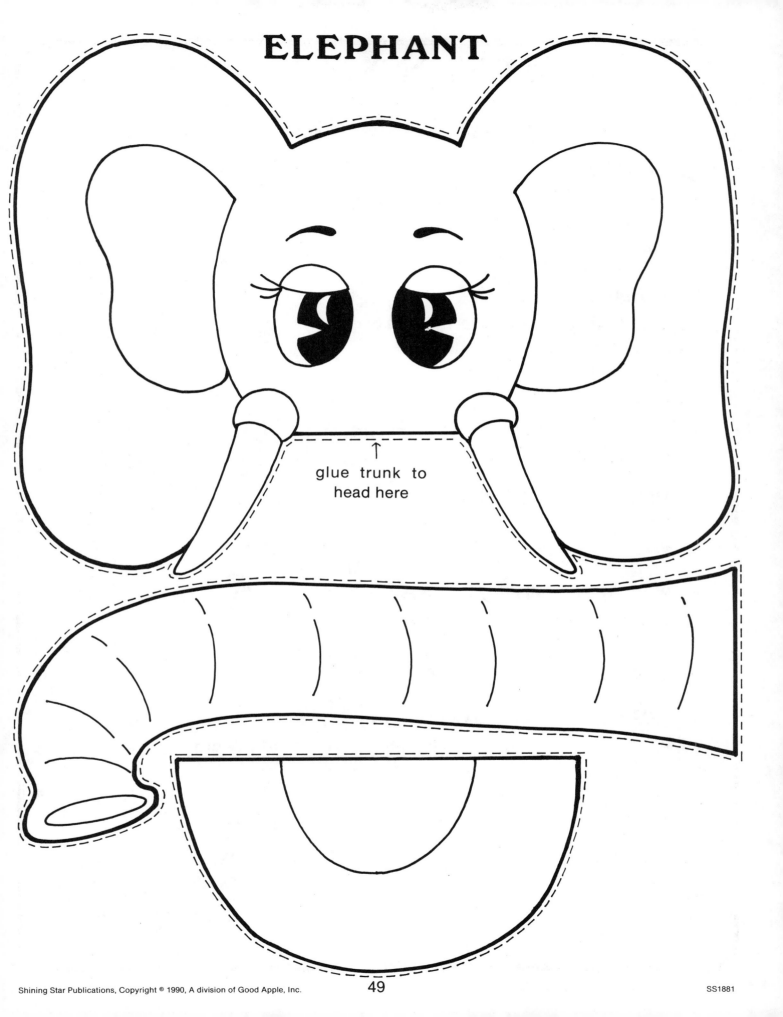

glue trunk to
head here

SS1881

ELEPHANT PUPPET

BIBLE STORIES:

The Garden of Eden (God Created Animals; The Animals Are Named) . . . Genesis 1:24-28; 2:19-20

Noah's Ark . . . Genesis 6-9:1-19

MATERIALS:

A Bible or children's Bible story/picture book

Copy of puppet head and mouth

Crayons or felt-tip marking pens

Scissors

Glue, gluestick, or paste

Lunch-size paper bag

Glue top of head here.

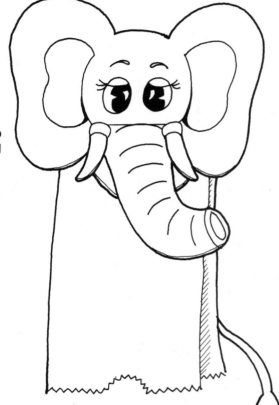

OPTIONAL MATERIALS:

Scrap of paper

Clear (Scotch) tape

HOW TO MAKE PUPPET:

1. Color the puppet's head and mouth.
2. Cut out the pieces.
3. Glue or paste the parts on the paper bag as shown in the picture.

OPTIONAL/SPECIAL INSTRUCTIONS:

Cut out a tail from paper or yarn and tape it to the back of the elephant.

Make two elephants for the Noah's Ark story.

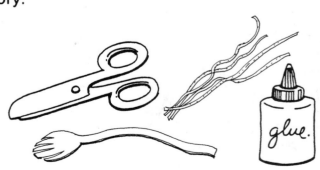

SS1881

ZEBRA

51

SS1881

ZEBRA PUPPET

BIBLE STORIES:

The Garden of Eden (God Created Animals; The Animals Are Named) . . .
Genesis 1:24-28; 2:19-20

Noah's Ark . . . Genesis 6-9:1-19

MATERIALS:

A Bible or children's Bible story/picture book

Copy of puppet head and mouth

Crayons or felt-tip marking pens

Scissors

Glue, gluestick, or paste

Lunch-size paper bag

OPTIONAL MATERIALS:

Scrap of paper

Black yarn

Clear (Scotch) tape

Glue top of head here.

HOW TO MAKE PUPPET:

1. Color the puppet's head and mouth.

2. Cut out the pieces.

3. Glue or paste the parts on the paper bag as shown in the picture.

OPTIONAL/SPECIAL INSTRUCTIONS:

Cut out a tail from paper or yarn and tape it to the back of the zebra.

Glue bits of yarn to the zebra's mane.

Make two zebras for the Noah's Ark story.

Shining Star Publications, Copyright © 1990, A division of Good Apple, Inc.

SS1881

COSTUME ACCESSORIES/ PROPS

GENERAL/OPTIONAL HINTS:

You may wish to glue all costume accessories and props onto heavy paper or cardboard to make them sturdier before cutting them out.

Tape the items to the puppets to change and remove them as needed to create different characters.

SHEPHERD'S HEADCOVERING AND STAFF:

Use these accessories with boys, and young or old men to make shepherds.

CROWN AND ANGEL'S ARMS:

Glue on glitter, sequins, foil scraps, or color with metallic-colored crayons or ink pens.

Use the angel accessories with young men or women puppets.

Fold and tape the center of the arms to the back of each angel puppet.

CHRISTMAS STAR:

Decorate with foil, glitter, and/or tinsel.

Tape to a stick or cardboard tube covered with foil to be the handle.

SAW/HAMMER:

Use these props to tell the story of when Noah built his ark (Genesis 6-9: 1-19).

FISH/LOAF OF BREAD:

Make five loaves of bread and 2 fish to tell the story of when Jesus used a boy's lunch to feed many people (John 6:1-14).

PALM BRANCH:

Color the palm branch green.

You may wish to cut other palm branches out of green paper to tell the Palm Sunday story (Matthew 21:1-11; Mark 11:1-10; Luke 19:28-38; John 12:12-15).

SS1881

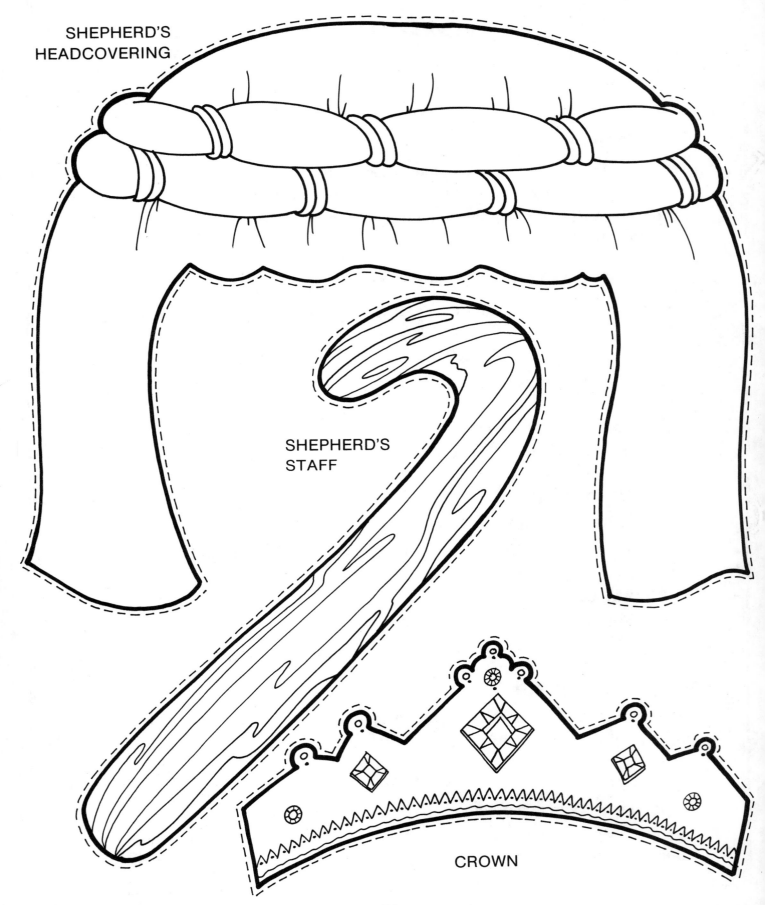

SHEPHERD'S
HEADCOVERING

SHEPHERD'S
STAFF

CROWN

SS1881

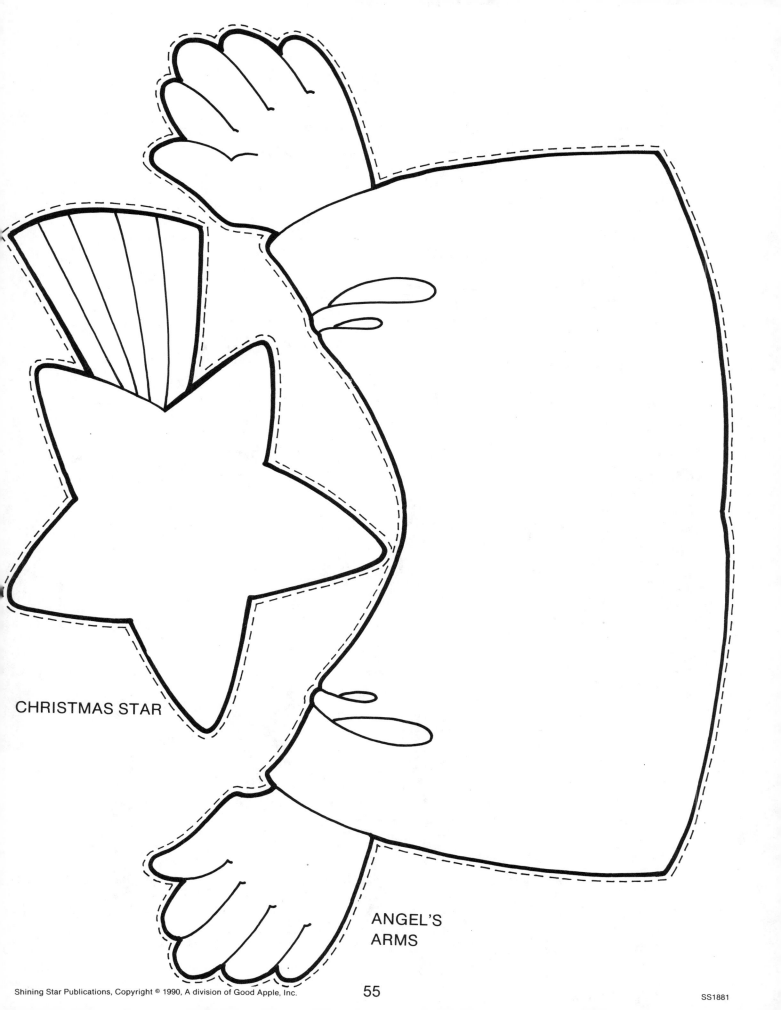

CHRISTMAS STAR

ANGEL'S
ARMS

55

SS1881

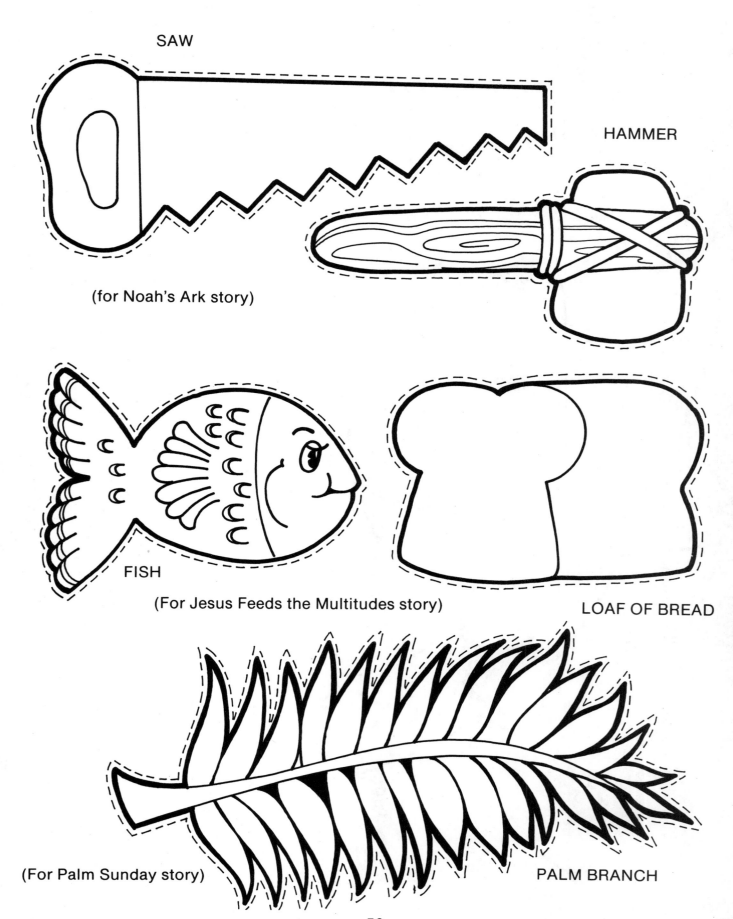

SAW

(for Noah's Ark story)

HAMMER

FISH

(For Jesus Feeds the Multitudes story)

LOAF OF BREAD

(For Palm Sunday story)

PALM BRANCH

CHOOSING PUPPETS TO DRAMATIZE OLD TESTAMENT STORIES

STORIES, SCRIPTURE REFERENCES, BIBLE CHARACTERS	PUPPETS	PROPS, ACCESSORIES (optional) See prop pages.	SCENERY (optional)
THE GARDEN OF EDEN (Genesis 1:24-31; 2:18-23; 4:2-3)			
Animals	All of the animals in book		Trees, plants (make from cardboard or use plastic flowers)
Adam	Young man		
Eve	Young woman		
Sons (Cain, Abel)	2 boys*		
NOAH'S ARK (Genesis 6-9:1-19)			
Noah	Old man	hammer	Ark (cut from cardboard)
Noah's wife	Old woman	saw	Waves (strips of blue paper)
Noah's sons (Shem, Ham, Japheth)	3 young men*		Rainbow (glue bands of colored paper or yarn onto cardboard backing; cotton clouds)
Noah's daughter-in-laws	3 young women*		
Animals	2 of each type of animal		

*Color and decorate each character to look different.

SS1881

CHOOSING PUPPETS TO DRAMATIZE OLD TESTAMENT STORIES

STORIES, SCRIPTURE REFERENCES, BIBLE CHARACTERS	PUPPETS	PROPS, ACCESSORIES (optional) See prop pages.	SCENERY (optional)
BABY MOSES IN THE BASKET (Exodus 2:1-10)			River (cut from blue paper) Reeds (put dried weeds in lumps of clay)
Baby Moses	Baby	Real basket	
Sister (Miriam)	Girl		
Moses' mother	Young woman*		
Pharaoh's daughter (princess)	Young woman*	Princess' crown	
Princess' attendants	Several young women*		
DAVID AND GOLIATH (I Samuel 17)			
David	Boy	Slingshot and stone (make from forked twig and large rubber band or elastic)	
David's father (Jesse)	Old man*		
King Saul	Old man*	King's crown	
Goliath	Giant (special puppet)		
	*Color and decorate each character to look different.		

SS1881

CHOOSING PUPPETS TO DRAMATIZE OLD TESTAMENT STORIES

STORIES, SCRIPTURE REFERENCES, BIBLE CHARACTERS	PUPPETS	PROPS, ACCESSORIES	SCENERY (optional)
THE LORD IS MY SHEPHERD (Psalm 23) Good Shepherd Sheep	Young or old man Sheep	Shepherd's headcovering Shepherd's staff	"Green pastures" (cut grass from green paper) "Still waters" (cut pond from blue paper)
DANIEL IN THE LION'S DEN (Daniel 6) Daniel King Darius Lions	Young man Old man Several lions	King's crown	

SS1881

CHOOSING PUPPETS TO DRAMATIZE NEW TESTAMENT STORIES

STORIES, SCRIPTURE REFERENCES, BIBLE CHARACTERS	PUPPETS	PROPS, ACCESSORIES (optional) See prop pages.	SCENERY (optional)
CHRISTMAS (JESUS' BIRTH) (Matthew 1-2; Luke 2:1-20)		Cover star with aluminum foil and silver glitter	Real straw or scraps of shredded yellow paper
Baby Jesus	Baby	Tinsel	
Mother (Mary)	Young woman*		
Joseph	Young man* (or older bearded man)	Star	Manger (cardboard box or small wooden crate)
Innkeeper	Old man	Stick or cardboard tube	
Shepherds	Young and old men*		
Angels	Young men or women*	Angel arms	
King Herod	Old man*	Shepherd's head-covering	
Wise men	3 young or old men*	Shepherd's staff	
Donkey	1 donkey	King and Wise men's crowns	
Sheep	Several sheep	3 tiny wrapped gifts (Wise men)	
Oxen (cattle)	Several cows		
Goat	1 or more goat(s)		
Camels	3 camels		
	*Color and decorate each character to look different.		

SS1881

CHOOSING PUPPETS TO DRAMATIZE NEW TESTAMENT STORIES

STORIES, SCRIPTURE REFERENCES, BIBLE CHARACTERS	PUPPETS	SCENERY (optional)
JESUS LOVES THE CHILDREN (Matthew 18:1-5; 19:13-15; Mark 9:33-37) Jesus .... Children .... Parents .... Disciples	Bearded man Several babies, boys, and girls* Young men and women* Young and older men*	
THE LOST SHEEP (Matthew 18:12-14) Shepherd or farmer .... Lost sheep	Young or old man Lamb	PROPS, ACCESSORIES (optional) See prop pages. Shepherd's head-covering Shepherd's staff *Color and decorate each character to look different.

SS1881

CHOOSING PUPPETS TO DRAMATIZE NEW TESTAMENT STORIES

STORIES, SCRIPTURE REFERENCES, BIBLE CHARACTERS	PUPPETS	PROPS, ACCESSORIES (optional) See prop pages.	SCENERY (optional)
THE PRODIGAL SON (Luke 15:11-32) Prodigal son Father Other son Swine	Young man*/teen Old man Young man* Pigs/hogs		
JESUS FEEDS THE MULTITUDE (John 6:1-14) Jesus Disciples Boy with lunch The "multitude"	Bearded man Several young men* Boy People of all ages* *Color and decorate each character to look different.	Lunch in basket (5 loaves of bread, 2 fish)	

SS1881

CHOOSING PUPPETS TO DRAMATIZE NEW TESTAMENT STORIES

STORIES, SCRIPTURE REFERENCES, BIBLE CHARACTERS	PUPPETS	PROPS, ACCESSORIES (optional) See prop pages.	SCENERY (optional)
PALM SUNDAY (Triumphal entry into Jerusalem) (Matthew 21:1-11; Mark 11:1-10; Luke 19: 28-38; John 12:12-15)	Jesus .... Bearded man 2 Disciples .... 2 young or old men* Crowd of people .... People of all ages* Donkey .... Donkey	Palm branches (color green or cut from green paper) Cloaks (scraps of fabric or doll clothing)	Road into Jerusalem (cut and tape together pieces of gray paper)
EASTER (Resurrection) (Matthew 28:1-10; Mark 16; Luke 24:1-12; John 20: 1-18)	Mary Magdalene .... Young woman Mary, Mother of Jesus .... Older woman Angel .... Young man or woman Jesus .... Bearded man	Angel arms	Large stone or cut a large circle from cardboard (a rock covered the tomb's entrance) Cardboard tomb background

*Color and decorate each character to look different.

Shining Star Publications, Copyright © 1990, A division of Good Apple, Inc.   SS1881

CERTIFICATE OF AWARD

presented to

_____

on _____

for puppetry.

_____
signature

SS1881